This Planner Belongs to

_____

School _____

Grade _____

Room _____

Address _____

_____

Email _____

Phone _____

Contacts
& Volunteers

Name	Contact Info

Welcome

Schedule

School Begins: _____

Lunch: _____ Recess: _____

Specials: _____

_____

School Ends: _____

Need Help?

Reliable Students: _____

Teachers: _____

Principal: _____

Vice Principal: _____

Other Staff: _____

Special Schedules

Name	Time/Location
_____	_____
_____	_____
_____	_____
_____	_____

Additional Notes

_____

_____

_____

_____

_____

Communication Log

DATE	TYPE	NAME	PURPOSE	NOTES
	📱 @ 🗏 👥			
	📱 @ 🗏 👥			
	📱 @ 🗏 👥			
	📱 @ 🗏 👥			
	📱 @ 🗏 👥			
	📱 @ 🗏 👥			
	📱 @ 🗏 👥			
	📱 @ 🗏 👥			
	📱 @ 🗏 👥			
	📱 @ 🗏 👥			
	📱 @ 🗏 👥			
	📱 @ 🗏 👥			
	📱 @ 🗏 👥			
	📱 @ 🗏 👥			
	📱 @ 🗏 👥			
	📱 @ 🗏 👥			
	📱 @ 🗏 👥			
	📱 @ 🗏 👥			
	📱 @ 🗏 👥			
	📱 @ 🗏 👥			
	📱 @ 🗏 👥			
	📱 @ 🗏 👥			
	📱 @ 🗏 👥			
	📱 @ 🗏 👥			
	📱 @ 🗏 👥			
	📱 @ 🗏 👥			

Communication Log

DATE	TYPE	NAME	PURPOSE	NOTES
	📱 @ 📋 👥			
	📱 @ 📋 👥			
	📱 @ 📋 👥			
	📱 @ 📋 👥			
	📱 @ 📋 👥			
	📱 @ 📋 👥			
	📱 @ 📋 👥			
	📱 @ 📋 👥			
	📱 @ 📋 👥			
	📱 @ 📋 👥			
	📱 @ 📋 👥			
	📱 @ 📋 👥			
	📱 @ 📋 👥			
	📱 @ 📋 👥			
	📱 @ 📋 👥			
	📱 @ 📋 👥			
	📱 @ 📋 👥			
	📱 @ 📋 👥			
	📱 @ 📋 👥			
	📱 @ 📋 👥			
	📱 @ 📋 👥			
	📱 @ 📋 👥			
	📱 @ 📋 👥			
	📱 @ 📋 👥			
	📱 @ 📋 👥			

News & Notes

News & Notes

What's up?

Plan It

Use these pages to create a classroom plan, record seating charts, create checklists, sketch plans, etc. The options are endless!

Year at a Glance

July

August

September

October

November

December

Year at a Glance

January

February

March

April

May

June

July

Sunday	Monday	Tuesday	Wednesday
○	○	○	○
○	○	○	○
○	○	○	○
○	○	○	○
○	○	○	○

Important Dates

_____

_____

_____

Goals

_____

_____

_____

Thursday	Friday	Saturday
○	○	○
○	○	○
○	○	○
○	○	○
○	○	○

Have To Do

○ _____

○ _____

○ _____

○ _____

○ _____

○ _____

○ _____

○ _____

○ _____

○ _____

○ _____

○ _____

Notes

_____

_____

_____

_____

_____

_____

_____

_____

_____

_____

_____

_____

_____

_____

PSST! USE THESE GUIDES TO KEEP YOUR TABS PERFECTLY PLACED.

August

Sunday	Monday	Tuesday	Wednesday
○	○	○	○
○	○	○	○
○	○	○	○
○	○	○	○
○	○	○	○

Important Dates

Goals

Thursday	Friday	Saturday	Have To Do
○	○	○	
○	○	○	
○	○	○	
○	○	○	
○	○	○	

Notes

September

Sunday	Monday	Tuesday	Wednesday
○	○	○	○
○	○	○	○
○	○	○	○
○	○	○	○
○	○	○	○

Important Dates

Goals

Thursday	Friday	Saturday	Have To Do

Have To Do

Notes

October

Sunday	Monday	Tuesday	Wednesday
◯	◯	◯	◯
◯	◯	◯	◯
◯	◯	◯	◯
◯	◯	◯	◯
◯	◯	◯	◯

Important Dates

Goals

Thursday	Friday	Saturday	Have To Do

Notes

November

Sunday	Monday	Tuesday	Wednesday
○	○	○	○
○	○	○	○
○	○	○	○
○	○	○	○
○	○	○	○

Important Dates

Goals

Thursday	Friday	Saturday	Have To Do
○	○	○	○ ————
			○ ————
			○ ————
○	○	○	○ ————
			○ ————
			○ ————
			○ ————
○	○	○	○ ————
			○ ————
			○ ————
○	○	○	○ ————
			○ ————

Notes

December

Sunday	Monday	Tuesday	Wednesday
○	○	○	○
○	○	○	○
○	○	○	○
○	○	○	○
○	○	○	○

Important Dates

Goals

Thursday	Friday	Saturday	Have To Do
◯	◯	◯	
◯	◯	◯	
◯	◯	◯	**Notes**
◯	◯	◯	
◯	◯	◯	

January

Sunday	Monday	Tuesday	Wednesday

Important Dates

Goals

Thursday	Friday	Saturday	Have To Do

Notes

February

Sunday	Monday	Tuesday	Wednesday
○	○	○	○
○	○	○	○
○	○	○	○
○	○	○	○
○	○	○	○

Important Dates

Goals

Thursday	Friday	Saturday	Have To Do

Notes

27

March

Sunday	Monday	Tuesday	Wednesday
○	○	○	○
○	○	○	○
○	○	○	○
○	○	○	○
○	○	○	○

Important Dates

Goals

Thursday	Friday	Saturday	Have To Do
○	○	○	○ _____
			○ _____
			○ _____
			○ _____
○	○	○	○ _____
			○ _____
			○ _____
			○ _____
			○ _____
			○ _____
			○ _____
○	○	○	**Notes**
			_____
○	○	○	_____
			_____
○	○	○	_____

April

Sunday	Monday	Tuesday	Wednesday
○	○	○	○
○	○	○	○
○	○	○	○
○	○	○	○
○	○	○	○

Important Dates

Goals

Thursday	Friday	Saturday	Have To Do

Notes

May

Sunday	Monday	Tuesday	Wednesday
○	○	○	○
○	○	○	○
○	○	○	○
○	○	○	○
○	○	○	○

Important Dates

Goals

Thursday	Friday	Saturday	Have To Do

Notes

June

Sunday	Monday	Tuesday	Wednesday
◯	◯	◯	◯
◯	◯	◯	◯
◯	◯	◯	◯
◯	◯	◯	◯
◯	◯	◯	◯

Important Dates

Goals

Thursday	Friday	Saturday	Have To Do
◯	◯	◯	
◯	◯	◯	
◯	◯	◯	Notes
◯	◯	◯	
◯	◯	◯	

WEEK

Subject	Subject	Subject

Mon. /

Tues. /

Wed. /

Thurs. /

Fri. /

Subject	Subject	Subject	Subject

PSST! CUT OFF THIS CORNER EACH WEEK TO MARK AND FIND YOUR PLACE EASILY.

WEEK

Subject	Subject	Subject

Mon. /

Tues. /

Wed. /

Thurs. /

Fri. /

Subject	Subject	Subject	Subject

WEEK

Subject	Subject	Subject

Mon.
/

Tues.
/

Wed.
/

Thurs.
/

Fri.
/

Subject	Subject	Subject	Subject

Subject	Subject	Subject

Mon.
/

Tues.
/

Wed.
/

Thurs.
/

Fri.
/

Subject	Subject	Subject	Subject

Subject	Subject	Subject

Mon.
/

Tues.
/

Wed.
/

Thurs.
/

Fri.
/

Subject	Subject	Subject	Subject

WEEK

Subject	Subject	Subject

Mon. /

Tues. /

Wed. /

Thurs. /

Fri. /

Subject	Subject	Subject	Subject

WEEK

Subject	Subject	Subject

Mon.
/

Tues.
/

Wed.
/

Thurs.
/

Fri.
/

Subject	Subject	Subject	Subject

WEEK

Subject	Subject	Subject

Mon. /

Tues. /

Wed. /

Thurs. /

Fri. /

Subject	Subject	Subject	Subject

WEEK

Subject	Subject	Subject

Mon. /

Tues. /

Wed. /

Thurs. /

Fri. /

Subject	Subject	Subject	Subject

WEEK

Subject	Subject	Subject

Mon. /

Tues. /

Wed. /

Thurs. /

Fri. /

54

Subject	Subject	Subject	Subject

Subject	Subject	Subject

Mon.
/

Tues.
/

Wed.
/

Thurs.
/

Fri.
/

Subject	Subject	Subject	Subject

Subject	Subject	Subject

Mon.
/

Tues.
/

Wed.
/

Thurs.
/

Fri.
/

Subject	Subject	Subject	Subject

WEEK

Subject	Subject	Subject

Mon. /

Tues. /

Wed. /

Thurs. /

Fri. /

Subject	Subject	Subject	Subject

WEEK

Subject	Subject	Subject

Mon.
/

Tues.
/

Wed.
/

Thurs.
/

Fri.
/

Subject	Subject	Subject	Subject

Subject	Subject	Subject

Mon.
/

Tues.
/

Wed.
/

Thurs.
/

Fri.
/

Subject	Subject	Subject	Subject

Subject	Subject	Subject

Mon.
/

Tues.
/

Wed.
/

Thurs.
/

Fri.
/

Subject	Subject	Subject	Subject

WEEK

Subject	Subject	Subject

Mon. /

Tues. /

Wed. /

Thurs. /

Fri. /

Subject	Subject	Subject	Subject

Subject	Subject	Subject

Mon.
/

Tues.
/

Wed.
/

Thurs.
/

Fri.
/

Subject	Subject	Subject	Subject

WEEK

Subject	Subject	Subject

Mon.
/

Tues.
/

Wed.
/

Thurs.
/

Fri.
/

Subject	Subject	Subject	Subject

WEEK

Subject	Subject	Subject

Mon. /

Tues. /

Wed. /

Thurs. /

Fri. /

Subject	Subject	Subject

Subject	Subject	Subject	Subject

WEEK

Subject	Subject	Subject

Mon. /

Tues. /

Wed. /

Thurs. /

Fri. /

Subject	Subject	Subject	Subject

WEEK

Subject	Subject	Subject

Mon. /

Tues. /

Wed. /

Thurs. /

Fri. /

Subject	Subject	Subject	Subject

WEEK#

Subject	Subject	Subject

Mon. /

Tues. /

Wed. /

Thurs. /

Fri. /

80

Subject	Subject	Subject	Subject

WEEK

Subject	Subject	Subject

Mon.
/

Tues.
/

Wed.
/

Thurs.
/

Fri.
/

Subject	Subject	Subject	Subject

Subject	Subject	Subject

Mon.
/

Tues.
/

Wed.
/

Thurs.
/

Fri.
/

Subject	Subject	Subject	Subject

WEEK

Subject	Subject	Subject

Mon.
/

Tues.
/

Wed.
/

Thurs.
/

Fri.
/

Subject	Subject	Subject	Subject

WEEK

Subject	Subject	Subject

Mon.
/

Tues.
/

Wed.
/

Thurs.
/

Fri.
/

Subject	Subject	Subject	Subject

Subject	Subject	Subject

Mon.
/

Tues.
/

Wed.
/

Thurs.
/

Fri.
/

Subject	Subject	Subject	Subject

Subject	Subject	Subject

Mon.
/

Tues.
/

Wed.
/

Thurs.
/

Fri.
/

Subject	Subject	Subject	Subject

WEEK#

Subject	Subject	Subject

Mon.
/

Tues.
/

Wed.
/

Thurs.
/

Fri.
/

Subject	Subject	Subject	Subject

Subject	Subject	Subject

Mon. /

Tues. /

Wed. /

Thurs. /

Fri. /

Subject	Subject	Subject	Subject

Subject	Subject	Subject

Mon.
/

Tues.
/

Wed.
/

Thurs.
/

Fri.
/

Subject	Subject	Subject	Subject

WEEK

Subject	Subject	Subject

Mon. /

Tues. /

Wed. /

Thurs. /

Fri. /

Subject	Subject	Subject	Subject

WEEK

Subject	Subject	Subject

Mon.
/

Tues.
/

Wed.
/

Thurs.
/

Fri.
/

Subject	Subject	Subject	Subject

WEEK

Subject	Subject	Subject

Mon. /

Tues. /

Wed. /

Thurs. /

Fri. /

Subject	Subject	Subject	Subject

Subject	Subject	Subject

Mon.
/

Tues.
/

Wed.
/

Thurs.
/

Fri.
/

Subject	Subject	Subject	Subject

Subject	Subject	Subject

Mon.
/

Tues.
/

Wed.
/

Thurs.
/

Fri.
/

Subject	Subject	Subject	Subject

WEEK

Subject	Subject	Subject

Mon. /

Tues. /

Wed. /

Thurs. /

Fri. /

Subject	Subject	Subject	Subject

WEEK

Subject	Subject	Subject

Mon.
/

Tues.
/

Wed.
/

Thurs.
/

Fri.
/

Subject	Subject	Subject	Subject

WEEK

Subject	Subject	Subject

Mon.
/

Tues.
/

Wed.
/

Thurs.
/

Fri.
/

Subject	Subject	Subject	Subject

Checklist

Name

Checklist

Name

PSST! CUT OFF THIS SECTION SO THAT YOU ONLY HAVE TO WRITE YOUR CLASS LIST ONCE.

Checklist

Name

Checklist

Name

Name

Checklist

Name

July July

August August

September September

October October

November November

December December

January January

February February

March March

April April

May May

June June

Checklists Checklists

Lesson Plans Lesson Plans

Conferences	Conferences	Staff Meeting	Staff Meeting	Professional Dev.
Conferences	Conferences	Staff Meeting	Staff Meeting	
Assembly	Early Release	Early Release	Early Release	Professional Dev.
Assembly	Early Release	Early Release	Early Release	
Holiday	Holiday	Holiday	Testing	Professional Dev.
Holiday	Holiday	Holiday	Testing	
No School	No School	No School	IEP Meeting	
No School	No School	No School	IEP Meeting	
Report Cards	Report Cards	Report Cards	Report Cards	

✶ TAKE NOTE

✶ PRIORITY

✶ DON'T FORGET

✶ TODAY

✶ GET IT DONE!

✶ BUSY DAY

Field Trip

Field Trip

Field Trip

PROGRESS REPORTS

PROGRESS REPORTS

PROGRESS REPORTS

PROGRESS REPORTS

Remember! Remember!
Remember! Remember!
Must Do! Must Do!
Must Do! Must Do!
Do This! Do This!
Do This! Do This!
Due: Due:
Due: Due:
Due: Due: